Amanda Lisetti

GENERATIONS REIMAGINED

The Complete Guide Uncovering
the Real Differences Between
Generation Z, Millennials,
Generation X, Boomers, Silents,
and Generation Alpha

To the man who forever changed my life, J.
But also to my Aunt Rose, my father, my mother, in no
particular order.
To myself, who always gave it my all, yes, to me too, why not?
This is a journey through the acknowledgments of different
generations that have taught me how to navigate the world
today.

WHO IS AMANDA LISETTI AND WHY SHOULD YOU READ THIS BOOK?

I am an Anglo-Italian journalist, born to an English mother and an Italian father.

I am a fusion of cultures, forever captivated by stories and the art of storytelling. Fascinated by people from an early age, I was born in the early '80s, just barely missing the cutoff for the Generation X (go ahead and do the math to figure out my exact birth year, consider it a little test), making me a proud member of Generation Y. Born in the UK, in Liverpool, I consider London my first and only home, alongside Milan and Rome. Well, technically the province of Rome.

In 2008, I obtained a master's degree in journalism in London, where I had a life-altering encounter with a man who completely transformed my path. As a result of that meeting, I started a blog, and with newfound ambition and audacity, I found myself working for The New York Times. I ended up being featured in several books, some of which I authored myself. It all started with one encounter, one hug. Perfect. The Perfect Hug.

I have stumbled and risen countless times, always remaining true to myself—stubborn, sometimes wrong, sometimes right. People have confirmed this about me. The truth is, I love being among people, telling their stories, immersing myself in their experiences. I relish being their reflection, the mirror of their stories to be shared with the world, for the world is hungry for stories, preferably beautiful ones.

Having encountered countless individuals throughout my journey, I have decided to write this book about generations. Primarily, it is a quest to learn how to contribute to you.

I lived in America for many years and had the opportunity to meet numerous individuals from different generational backgrounds and origins while writing articles as a freelancer or for magazines, newspapers, and blogs. Even after no longer residing permanently in America, I returned on multiple occasions with the intention of studying not only the American generations but also to compare behaviors and ways of being with the "Generations" across the world. I have traveled extensively, for work, for pleasure, for the thrill of it.

I have faced countless situations that have shaped me—tenacious, free-spirited, with the wind in my hair, unencumbered by constraints, without regrets. I have no regrets about any of my experiences, despite the ups and downs of my life. With all the accumulated knowledge and experience, I haven't simply focused on discussing the American Generations. At the end of this book, you will find an exploration of what generations have accomplished in Europe, Asia, Africa, and the Middle East.

My goal was to examine if there was a common thread connecting the way of thinking based on the historical period of birth, transcending generations worldwide. Of course, it is impossible to generalize and categorize all individuals born within a certain timeframe as a single unified group.

However, it is valuable to observe that certain behaviors and patterns of thought and action have proved remarkably similar across time and space.

Perhaps this could serve as a subject of study for my future books.

In essence, this book explores the generations of America and beyond. I have employed my experiences to better understand one of the most enchanting and incredible countries in the world.

Given the places I have lived, even briefly, the people I have encountered, and the observed behavioral patterns, I couldn't limit myself to just talking about America. Today, this could be one of the most comprehensive works of research, essays, and exposition on the generations of the past 100 years worldwide. Don't miss out on it.

Embark on a captivating journey through the generations of the past two centuries.

Let us delve into the intricacies of these generational shifts together.

Amanda

INTRODUCTION

From the Silent Generation to Gen Z, America has seen significant social, cultural, and technological changes that have shaped the values, attitudes, and behaviors of each generation. But where did these generational divisions come from?

Who invented them? And why do they matter?

In this book, we'll explore the history and significance of generational divisions, delving into the forces that shaped each cohort and the impact that they have had on American society. We'll also look at the unique challenges and opportunities that each generation faces, and how they can work together to create a better future for all.

But first, let's take a step back and look at how generational divisions came to be. While the concept of different age groups with unique characteristics and values is not new, it was not until the 20th century that it became widely recognized and studied.

The first attempt to define generational cohorts came in the 1920s, when demographers William Strauss and Neil Howe identified four distinct generations that they believed had shaped American history. They called these generations the G.I. Generation (born 1901-1924), the Silent Generation (born 1925-1942), the Baby Boomers (born 1943-1960), and Generation X (born 1961-1981).

Since then, other researchers and commentators have added or revised generational cohorts, such as the Millennials (born 1982-1996) and Gen Z (born 1997-2012). While the exact dates and names of these generations may vary depending on the source, the basic idea remains the same: different age groups have unique characteristics that define their experiences and perspectives.

So why is it important to make these distinctions? One reason is that understanding generational differences can help us navigate social, economic, and political change. By recognizing the experiences and values of each cohort, we can better understand their perspectives and work together to address common challenges.

Another reason is that generational divisions can also shape social identity and cultural norms. From the rebellious counterculture of the Baby Boomers to the digital native identity of Gen Z, each generation has contributed to a collective identity that shapes how we see ourselves and our society.

In this book, we'll explore each generation in detail, from the events that shaped their formative years to the values and attitudes that define their worldview. We'll also examine how generational differences play out in areas such as politics, technology, and work, and what implications these differences have for our collective future.

But while we will be exploring the unique characteristics of each generation, it's important to remember that not all members of a generation will share the same experiences or perspectives. Generational divisions are not deterministic, and individual differences such as race, gender, and socioeconomic status can have a significant impact on a person's life and worldview.

With this in mind, let's dive into the world of generational differences and explore what each cohort brings to the table. From the Silent Generation to Gen Z, we'll examine the forces that shaped each generation and how they are shaping the future of America.

THE FIRST 'GENERATIONS' BOOK

Let's start by the beginning. "Generations: The History of America's Future, 1584 to 2069" is a groundbreaking book written by William Strauss and Neil Howe, which was published in 1992. This extensive work presents a comprehensive analysis of generational theory and its profound impact on American history and society. With its thought-provoking insights and compelling predictions, "Generations" sparked a significant shift in American public opinion and had a lasting influence on various aspects of society.

At the core of "Generations" is the central thesis that history unfolds in a series of recurring generational cycles, each with its distinct characteristics, values, and attitudes. Strauss and Howe identified four archetypal generational types: Idealist, Reactive, Civic, and Adaptive generations, and proposed that these cycles repeat approximately every 80 years, known as a "saeculum." By examining the patterns and dynamics of generational cohorts from the Colonial Era to the present day, the authors provided a compelling framework for understanding societal changes, political shifts, and cultural transformations.

One of the key impacts of "Generations" was its profound influence on public perception and awareness of generational differences. The book shed light on why different generations possess unique values, beliefs, and attitudes, emphasizing the importance of generational experiences in shaping the course of history. This new perspective resonated with the American public, as it provided a framework for understanding the generational dynamics that underpin social, political, and cultural developments.

The release of "Generations" marked a turning point in the study of generational theory, leading to renewed interest and further research across multiple disciplines. Scholars, policymakers, and marketers began to delve deeper into generational dynamics, exploring how generational cohorts impact society, economics, and consumer behavior. The book's insights revolutionized the understanding of generational differences, challenging prevailing stereotypes and fostering a more nuanced understanding of intergenerational interactions.

Moreover, "Generations" had a significant impact on the political landscape. The book prompted politicians and strategists to consider generational factors in their campaign strategies and policy-making decisions. Recognizing the distinct values and priorities of different generations became crucial for politicians aiming to connect with specific voter segments. The framework provided by "Generations" enabled politicians to tailor their messages and policies to resonate with the concerns and aspirations of various generational cohorts.

The influence of "Generations" extended beyond academia and politics, permeating popular culture and everyday conversations. Discussions about generational dynamics became more prevalent, and the book's concepts and terminology entered the public lexicon. The profound impact of generational differences on societal trends and cultural shifts became a topic of interest and exploration across various media platforms.

Furthermore, "Generations" proved prescient in its predictions about the Millennial generation, which was still in its infancy at the time of the book's publication. The authors accurately anticipated that Millennials would wield significant influence and reshape various aspects of society, including technology, politics, and the economy. As these predictions began to materialize, the credibility and relevance of "Generations" were reinforced, further solidifying its impact on public opinion.

So, "Generations: The History of America's Future, 1584 to 2069" by William Strauss and Neil Howe revolutionized the understanding of generational dynamics in American society. This seminal work provided a compelling framework for comprehending the cyclical nature of history and the profound influence of generational cohorts. By shedding light on the distinct values, attitudes, and experiences of different generations, "Generations" transformed public opinion and sparked discussions that continue to shape our understanding of societal change. Its enduring impact can be seen in the increased recognition and analysis of generational differences in academia, politics, and popular culture. The book's extensive analysis and insightful predictions captured the imagination of the American public, sparking a shift in how generational dynamics are perceived and understood.

"Generations" not only provided valuable insights into the past and present but also offered a framework for predicting future societal trends. The authors' projections about the Millennial generation, in particular, have proven remarkably accurate. They anticipated that Millennials would be a transformative force, leveraging technology to reshape industries, driving social and political change, and challenging traditional norms and institutions. As the Millennial generation came of age and exerted its influence, the predictions put forth in "Generations" gained credibility and reinforced the book's impact on public opinion.

The influence of "Generations" extended beyond academia and resonated with a broad audience. The book became a touchstone for understanding the dynamics of generational cohorts and their impact on society. It provided a common language and framework for discussions about generational differences, enabling individuals and groups to better understand their own generational identities and appreciate the perspectives of other generations. The book's concepts and terminology entered the public consciousness, enriching public discourse and fostering a deeper appreciation for the diverse experiences and viewpoints across generations.

"Generations" also spurred further research and exploration of generational dynamics across various disciplines. Scholars, sociologists, and psychologists delved deeper into the subject, building upon the foundational work laid out in the book. The framework presented by Strauss and Howe in "Generations" continues to shape and inform research on generational theory, offering valuable insights into societal shifts, cultural developments, and intergenerational interactions.

In addition to its intellectual impact, "Generations" had tangible effects on marketing and business strategies. Marketers recognized the significance of generational cohorts as distinct consumer segments, each with its unique preferences, values, and purchasing behaviors. Understanding generational dynamics became essential for businesses seeking to connect with their target audiences and tailor their products and messaging accordingly. The book provided marketers with a roadmap for engaging different generations effectively, unlocking new avenues for growth and success.

Overall, "Generations: The History of America's Future, 1584 to 2069" by William Strauss and Neil Howe had a profound impact on American public opinion. It revolutionized the understanding of generational dynamics, providing a comprehensive framework for comprehending the cyclical nature of history and the profound influence of generational cohorts. The book's insights and predictions resonated with the public, stimulating discussions, shaping public discourse, and influencing various aspects of society, from politics and culture to business and marketing. Its enduring legacy continues to shape our understanding of generational differences and their impact on the trajectory of society.

William Strauss, co-author of "Generations: The History of America's Future, 1584 to 2069," was an American historian and writer born in 1947. Alongside his co-author Neil Howe, Strauss made significant contributions to the field of generational theory and its application in understanding American history and society. The publication of "Generations" in 1992 marked a pivotal moment in American intellectual and cultural discourse, as it emerged during a period of social and political transformation.

At the time of writing "Generations," the United States was undergoing a profound shift in its social and political landscape. The late 20th century witnessed the end of the Cold War, the collapse of the Soviet Union, and the emergence of the United States as the world's sole superpower. These seismic global events had far-reaching implications for American society, as they coincided with significant domestic changes.

In the 1980s and early 1990s, the country experienced a renewed sense of optimism and economic growth, characterized by President Ronald Reagan's conservative policies and the subsequent presidency of George H.W. Bush. However, beneath the surface, social and cultural fault lines were becoming more apparent. Issues such as racial tensions, economic inequality, and political polarization were intensifying, foreshadowing the challenges that would shape the coming decades.

It was within this context that William Strauss and Neil Howe embarked on their ambitious project to analyze the patterns of American history through a generational lens. Drawing from their expertise in history and sociology, the authors sought to provide a comprehensive understanding of how generational cohorts shape society and influence its trajectory. Their work aimed to illuminate the cyclical nature of history and the recurring patterns that emerge as generations rise and fall.

Strauss and Howe's research was informed by historical events and the experiences of various generations, spanning from the Colonial Era to the present day. By examining how each generation responded to and influenced societal shifts, they identified recurring patterns and archetypes that helped explain the dynamics of American history. Their goal was not only to analyze the past but also to make predictions about future generational cycles, offering insights into what lay ahead for American society.

"Generations" presented a compelling narrative that resonated with readers, as it provided a framework for understanding the challenges and opportunities facing contemporary America. It offered a fresh perspective on the interconnectedness of generations and the ways in which they shape cultural, political, and social developments. The book's historical context was a reflection of the times, capturing the zeitgeist of a nation undergoing profound change.

Strauss and Howe's work had a profound impact on public discourse and intellectual debates. It encouraged a deeper examination of generational dynamics and their influence on society, challenging prevailing assumptions and stereotypes. The book prompted individuals from various fields, including academia, politics, and business, to consider the implications of generational theory in their respective domains.

In the political realm, the ideas presented in "Generations" had significant implications. Politicians and strategists began to recognize the importance of generational factors in understanding public sentiment and crafting effective messaging. The book provided valuable insights into the values, beliefs, and aspirations of different generations, helping political campaigns tailor their appeals to resonate with specific voter segments.

Beyond politics, "Generations" also had an impact on popular culture and the broader public. It sparked conversations about generational differences, fostering a greater appreciation for the diverse experiences and perspectives of various age groups. The book's concepts and terminology became part of the cultural lexicon, permeating discussions about societal trends, cultural shifts, and intergenerational dynamics.

William Strauss, drawing from his background as a historian, brought a deep understanding of American history to the project. His expertise allowed him to contextualize the generational dynamics within broader historical narratives and highlight the recurring patterns that shaped the nation's trajectory. By examining the experiences, values, and attitudes of different generations, Strauss illuminated the ways in which they influenced social, cultural, and political developments.

Strauss and Howe's work was significant not only for its historical analysis but also for its predictive power. The book's exploration of generational cycles and its projections about the future resonated with readers seeking to make sense of the changing world around them. In particular, their predictions about the Millennial generation and its potential for transformative change captured the imagination of many.

The publication of "Generations" in 1992 coincided with a period of introspection and soul-searching for the United States. The country was grappling with economic uncertainties, social tensions, and a sense of cultural fragmentation. The book's insights into the generational dynamics provided a framework for understanding these challenges and offered hope for navigating the complexities of a rapidly evolving society.

One of the notable impacts of "Generations" was its influence on public opinion and discourse. The book sparked conversations and debates about the role of generations in shaping the nation's destiny. It prompted individuals to reflect on their own generational identities and fostered a deeper appreciation for the diverse perspectives and experiences across age groups.

Furthermore, the concepts and terminology introduced in "Generations" had practical applications beyond academia. The book influenced marketing and business strategies, as companies recognized the significance of generational cohorts as distinct consumer segments. Understanding generational dynamics became crucial for businesses seeking to connect with their target audiences and tailor their products and messages accordingly.

In summary, William Strauss's work in co-authoring "Generations" with Neil Howe had a profound impact on American public opinion. The book's historical context, set against the backdrop of social and political transformations, contributed to its significance. By offering a comprehensive framework for understanding generational dynamics, Strauss and Howe's work influenced public discourse, political campaigns, marketing strategies, and cultural conversations. The enduring legacy of "Generations" continues to shape our understanding of the interplay between generations and their profound impact on the trajectory of American society.

In conclusion, William Strauss and Neil Howe's "Generations" emerged during a transformative period in American history, capturing the social and political shifts that were reshaping the nation. Their work provided a thought-provoking framework for understanding the cyclical nature of history and the profound influence of generational cohorts. The book's historical context, set against the backdrop of the end of the Cold War and the changing socio-political landscape of the late 20th century, contributed to its impact and resonance.

WHERE ARE WE GOING?

"Generations Reimagined: The Complete Guide Uncovering the Real Differences Between Generation Z, Millennials, Generation X, Boomers, Silents, and Generation Alpha" is a book that has the scope of Unlocking the Power of Generational Shifts and Embracing the Rise of Gen Alpha.

We will embark on a captivating journey through time, exploring the profound impact of different generations on our world. From the resilient Silent Generation to the trailblazing Baby Boomers, the independent Gen X, the tech-savvy Millennials, and the socially conscious Gen Z, each generation has left an indelible mark on history.

As we turn our attention to the future, we find ourselves on the brink of a transformative era with the emergence of Generation Alpha. Born into a world characterized by unprecedented technological advancements, global connectivity, and pressing environmental challenges, Gen Alpha represents the next wave of change. With their innate digital fluency, natural adaptability, and boundless potential, they are poised to reshape our world in ways we can only begin to imagine.

But what does the future hold for our children, the Gen Alpha? How can we prepare them for the challenges and opportunities that lie ahead? In this thought-provoking exploration, we delve into the present realities and the potential futures of Gen Alpha. Drawing from real data, research, and expert insights, we unravel the characteristics, aspirations, and unique strengths of this emerging generation.

However, our journey is not confined to the future alone. To truly understand the path that lies ahead, we must first acknowledge the lessons and legacies of the past. We delve into the pivotal moments and defining traits of each preceding generation, recognizing the threads that connect us and the wisdom we can glean from their experiences.

"Generations Reimagined" is not just a nostalgic trip down memory lane, nor is it a crystal ball predicting an uncertain future. It is a compelling exploration of the interplay between generations, the present landscape we navigate, and the possibilities that await us.

By understanding the distinct perspectives, values, and motivations of each generation, we can bridge divides, foster empathy, and harness the collective power to create a better future.

Join us on this enlightening journey as we unravel the intricacies of generational dynamics, celebrate the triumphs of the past, embrace the present moment, and ignite the imagination for the world Gen Alpha will inherit.

Let us chart a course that honors our diverse legacies while forging a path toward a brighter tomorrow.

Together, let's reimagine the generations and unlock the transformative potential of Gen Alpha.

Silent Generation to Gen Z, America has seen significant social, cultural, and technological changes that have shaped the values, attitudes, and behaviors of each generation.

But where did these generational divisions come from?

Who invented them?

And why do they matter?

Let's discover more together.

WHO DID THIS THE FIRST TIME?

It's difficult to pinpoint a specific person who first put all these generational terms together, as it's a concept that has evolved over time with input from various sources. However, the idea of categorizing people into different generational groups based on shared experiences and values can be traced back to the work of social scientists and demographers who studied population trends and cohort effects.

One of the earliest proponents of this approach was the sociologist Karl Mannheim, who in the 1920s proposed the concept of "generational units" to describe the shared experiences and perspectives of people born during certain historical periods. Later, in the 1960s and 1970s, researchers such as Neil Howe and William Strauss developed the concept of "generational cycles" based on recurring patterns of social, political, and economic change.

The terms Baby Boomers, Generation X, and Millennials were popularized in the 1980s and 1990s by cultural critics and journalists who were trying to

24

make sense of the cultural and political shifts of those decades. The term Gen Z emerged more recently, as the cohort born after the Millennials began to enter adulthood and gain cultural prominence.

While it's difficult to pinpoint a single person or source that first put together all the generations' definitions, it is believed that the concept of generational cohorts and their unique characteristics was popularized by William Strauss and Neil Howe in their 1991 book "Generations: The History of America's Future, 1584 to 2069." Their book examines the recurring patterns in American history and how generational differences shape these patterns. Since then, the concept of generational cohorts and their defining characteristics has been widely used and discussed in various fields, including sociology, marketing, and business.

Generations examines American history through the lens of generational cycles, dividing the population into four generational archetypes: the Idealist, Reactive, Civic, and Adaptive generations.

The authors argue that these archetypes repeat throughout American history, and that each generation's formative experiences shape their values, attitudes, and behaviors in distinct ways. They also suggest that the interactions between these generations can have significant effects on American politics, culture, and society.

The book had a significant impact on media and popular culture, as it popularized the idea of generational theory and introduced terms like Baby Boomers, Generation X, and Millennials to a wider audience. It also influenced political and business leaders, who used the insights from the book to better understand and engage with different generations.

In the years following the book's publication, discussions of generations and generational theory became more common in the media and in academic circles.

Today, the idea that different generations have distinct values, beliefs, and behaviors is widely accepted and continues to shape our understanding of American society.

THE SILENT GENERATION

The term "Silent Generation" was coined by Time magazine in a 1951 cover story titled "The Younger Generation," which was written by journalist William Strauss. In the article, Strauss referred to the generation born between 1925 and 1942 as the "Silent Generation" because he believed that they had been overshadowed by the preceding "Greatest Generation" and the following Baby Boomers.

Strauss argued that the Silent Generation had grown up in a time of economic and social upheaval, with the Great Depression and World War II shaping their experiences and attitudes. He suggested that they were a cautious and conservative group, marked by a sense of duty and conformity, and lacking the rebellious spirit of the Baby Boomers who would follow them.

The term "Silent Generation" caught on and has since become a widely recognized way of referring to the cohort of Americans born during this period. It is worth noting, however, that not everyone agrees with the characterization of the Silent Generation as silent or lacking in influence. Some historians and commentators have pointed out that members of this generation played important roles in shaping American society and culture, from the civil rights movement to the rise of rock and roll.

In this chapter, we'll explore the generation that came of age during the Great Depression and World War II. We'll examine the values and characteristics that define the Silent Generation, such as their strong sense of duty, conformity, and deference to authority. We'll also look at how their experiences shaped their attitudes toward work, family, and politics, and what implications these values have for America's future.

The Silent Generation, also known as the "Lucky Few," is the cohort born between 1928 and 1945, and they came of age during some of the most tumultuous times in American history. This generation was born into an era of economic instability, social upheaval, and war. They are sandwiched between the Greatest Generation, who fought in World War II, and the Baby Boomers, who came of age in the post-war boom. Despite being overshadowed by these two iconic generations, the Silent Generation played a vital role in shaping America's future.

The Silent Generation was born into an era of economic hardship. The Great Depression began in 1929, when the stock market crashed, and lasted for a decade. Unemployment rates soared, and many families struggled to make ends meet. As a result, the Silent Generation learned the value of hard work and frugality. They were often described as "savers," as they were taught to save their money and avoid debt.

The Silent Generation also experienced World War II, which had a profound impact on their lives. Many of them were drafted into military service, or knew someone who was. They witnessed the sacrifices that their parents and older siblings made in the war effort, and this instilled in them a sense of duty and patriotism. The war also brought about social changes, as women entered the workforce in large numbers to replace the men who had gone to war.

After the war, the Silent Generation entered a period of economic prosperity. The post-war boom saw the rise of the middle class, and many Silent Generation members were able to achieve a level of financial stability that their parents had never known. This economic stability gave them the opportunity to start families, buy homes, and pursue their dreams.

However, the Silent Generation was also shaped by the social and political changes of the time. The Civil Rights Movement, the Cold War, and the Vietnam War all had a profound impact on their worldview. The Silent Generation grew up in a time when segregation was the norm, and they witnessed the struggle for civil rights firsthand. They also came of age during the Cold War, when the threat of nuclear war loomed large, and many of them protested the Vietnam War.

Despite these challenges, the Silent Generation is often characterized by their sense of conformity and deference to authority. They were taught to respect their elders and authority figures, and to conform to social norms. This tendency toward conformity has led some to describe the Silent Generation as "risk-averse" and "cautious."

In terms of their contributions to American society, the Silent Generation has made significant contributions in fields such as science, technology, and the arts. This generation includes luminaries such as Neil Armstrong, Elvis Presley, and Martin Luther King Jr. They also played a significant role in shaping American politics, with notable members such as Jimmy Carter and John McCain.

Looking to the future, the Silent Generation's values of hard work, duty, and conformity have implications for America's future. As they retire and pass on, their influence will be felt in the values they instilled in their children and grandchildren. The Silent Generation has played a vital role in shaping America's history, and their legacy will continue to shape its future.

This generation came of age during some of the most challenging times in American history, including the Great Depression and World War II. Their experiences shaped their values and attitudes toward work, family, and politics, and their contributions to American society have been significant. While they are often overshadowed by the Greatest Generation and the Baby Boomers, the Silent Generation played a vital role in shaping America's future, and their influence will be felt for generations to come.

Basing on my studies, this is an overview of the impact The Silent Generation had on work, mindset, life expectations, traveling and medicine.

A. Work: The Silent Generation's strong sense of duty and work ethic helped shape America's post-war economic boom. Many Silent Generation members pursued stable, long-term careers, often with a single company. This generation's commitment to hard work and loyalty helped establish a foundation for future prosperity.

B. Mindset: The Silent Generation's conformity and deference to authority helped maintain a sense of stability and order in post-war America. However, this mindset also contributed to a lack of questioning and resistance to social and political change, which would become a defining feature of later generations.

C. Life Expectations: The Silent Generation experienced significant improvements in life expectancy and quality of life thanks to advancements in medicine and healthcare. This, combined with the post-war economic boom, helped create a sense of optimism and prosperity for this generation.

D. Traveling: While travel was not as accessible or popular during the Silent Generation's early years, advancements in transportation technology and infrastructure during their lifetime helped make travel more accessible and affordable. This, coupled with their sense of duty to explore the world and experience new things, helped pave the way for future generations' love of travel.

E. Medicine: The Silent Generation witnessed incredible advancements in medicine, including the development of antibiotics and vaccines, which helped save countless lives and improve overall health outcomes. This, combined with their sense of duty and responsibility, helped establish a strong foundation for future progress in medical research and care.

The Silent Generation grew up during a time of great social and economic upheaval, and their experiences helped to shape their values and beliefs. In this section, we will discuss some of the most significant changes that the Silent Generation brought to America.

Economic growth and prosperity:
The Silent Generation came of age during a time of unprecedented economic growth and prosperity in America. The postwar boom created new opportunities for employment and wealth accumulation, and the Silent Generation was able to take advantage of these opportunities. The economy was expanding rapidly, and the Silent Generation was able to enjoy the benefits of this growth.

Civil rights movement:
The S.G. also played a significant role in the civil rights movement. This generation witnessed the struggle for equal rights for African Americans and

other minorities and worked to make a difference. They were the ones who marched for desegregation, voter rights, and equal opportunities. The Silent Generation helped to lay the groundwork for the civil rights movement that would continue through the 1960s.

Technological advancements:
And, of course, this generation witnessed some of the most significant technological advancements of the 20th century. They saw the rise of television, the development of the internet, and the growth of the computer industry. These technological advancements transformed the way people lived and worked, and the Silent Generation helped to drive these changes.

Cultural shifts:
The Silent Generation was responsible for some significant cultural shifts in America. They were the ones who embraced rock and roll music and popularized the idea of youth culture. They challenged traditional gender roles and helped to pave the way for the feminist movement. They were also responsible for a greater emphasis on individualism and personal expression.

Shifts in family structures:
The S.G. saw significant shifts in family structures. They were the ones who experienced the rise of the nuclear family and the decline of extended family networks. They were also the first generation to see a significant increase in divorce rates, which had a profound impact on children and families.

Cold War tensions:

These 'people' grew up during the height of the Cold War, and their experiences shaped their attitudes toward war and international relations. They witnessed the arms race between the United States and the Soviet Union, the Cuban Missile Crisis, and the Vietnam War. These experiences influenced their views on foreign policy, defense, and international relations.

Advances in medicine:

They also saw significant advances in medical technology and treatments. They witnessed the development of antibiotics, the introduction of vaccines, and the growth of medical research. These medical advancements improved the quality of life for millions of Americans and helped to reduce the impact of infectious diseases.

So, this generation had a significant impact on America in the postwar era. They witnessed unprecedented economic growth, technological advancements, and social and cultural changes. They played a critical role in the civil rights movement and helped to shape America's cultural and political landscape.

Their experiences also helped to lay the groundwork for the generations that followed, including the Baby Boomers, Generation X, Millennials, and Gen Z.

The Silent Generation's legacy is one of resilience, hard work, and dedication, and their impact on

America will continue to be felt for generations to come.

The term "The Silent Generation" was coined to describe a specific group of people in the United States, but its impact has extended beyond America and into other countries.

Here are some of the ways that this generation has influenced the world:

Post-World War II reconstruction: The Silent Generation played a critical role in rebuilding Europe and Japan after World War II. They were the ones who worked hard to rebuild homes, infrastructure, and economies, which helped to create a new era of prosperity and stability around the world.

Social welfare programs: The Silent Generation also played a significant role in creating social welfare programs that helped to provide support for the elderly, the sick, and the poor. Programs like Social Security and Medicare were established during this time, which helped to provide a safety net for millions of people.

Environmentalism: The Silent Generation also helped to raise awareness about environmental issues and the need for conservation. This led to the creation of the Environmental Protection Agency (EPA) in the United States, as well as other environmental regulations around the world.

Civil rights: The Civil Rights Movement was another major social movement that was led by members of the Silent Generation. They played a significant role in ending segregation and discrimination against African Americans, which paved the way for greater equality and social justice in the United States and around the world.

Literature and arts: Members of the Silent Generation also had a significant impact on literature and the arts. Many of the most influential writers and artists of the 20th century, such as Allen Ginsberg, Jack Kerouac, and Robert Rauschenberg, were members of this generation.

It's difficult to pinpoint exactly when other countries started using the term "The Silent Generation," but it is likely that the term was adopted in other countries shortly after it was popularized in the United States. The impact of this generation has been felt around the world in a variety of ways, and it will continue to be felt for many years to come.

BABY BOOMERS

The term "Baby Boomers" was coined by Landon Jones, an American writer and editor, in a 1980 article in Time magazine. Jones was born in 1942, making him a member of the Baby Boomer generation himself. In 1980, Jones wrote an article for Time magazine titled "The Year of the Baby Boomer," in which he used the term to describe the large cohort of Americans born between 1946 and 1964. The term quickly caught on and has since become a widely recognized way of referring to this generation.

In his article, Jones noted that the Baby Boomers were a generation that was "changing the rules" in American society. He cited their impact on the economy, politics, and culture, and suggested that their sheer numbers were a driving force behind their influence. Jones also noted that the Baby Boomers were a diverse group, with a wide range of values, beliefs, and attitudes, but he argued that they shared a common sense of idealism and a desire to make a difference in the world.

The Baby Boomers are the generation born between 1946 and 1964, following the end of World War II. They represent a significant demographic shift in American society, with approximately 76 million people born during this period. The term "baby boom" was coined due to the significant increase in birth rates during this time, which was largely attributed to the return of soldiers from war and a strong post-war economic boom.

Historical Context:
The Baby Boomer generation was raised during a time of economic prosperity and social change. After World War II, America experienced an unprecedented economic boom that lasted well into the 1960s. This period of prosperity helped create a strong middle class and provided opportunities for many Baby Boomers to pursue higher education and professional careers.

The 1960s and 1970s were a time of significant social and cultural change, marked by the civil rights movement, the women's rights movement, and the counterculture movement. Baby Boomers were at the forefront of many of these movements, advocating for social justice, equality, and individual freedom.

Characteristics:
The Baby Boomers are often characterized as idealistic, ambitious, and individualistic. They were raised during a time of prosperity and opportunity,

which instilled in them a belief that anything was possible. They value personal growth and self-expression, and often prioritize their own needs over the needs of the group.

Work:

Baby Boomers are known for their strong work ethic and dedication to their careers. Many pursued high-paying jobs in fields such as finance, law, and medicine, and were willing to work long hours to achieve success. They also valued job security and often stayed with a single company for long periods of time.

Family:

The Baby Boomer generation witnessed significant changes in family structure and dynamics. The divorce rate increased during this period, and many Baby Boomers grew up in single-parent households. However, they also placed a high value on family and were committed to providing their own children with a stable, nurturing environment.

Politics:

The Baby Boomers were deeply involved in politics, both as activists and as voters. They were at the forefront of many social and political movements, advocating for civil rights, women's rights, and environmental protection. They also had a significant impact on American politics, with many Baby Boomers holding positions of power in government and business.

Impact:

The Baby Boomers have had a significant impact on American society, culture, and politics. Their idealism and commitment to personal growth helped shape the counterculture movement and led to significant social and cultural change. They also helped establish a strong middle class and created new opportunities for future generations.

However, their individualistic mindset has also contributed to a sense of entitlement and a lack of concern for the needs of the group. This, combined with their large numbers and political power, has contributed to a sense of political gridlock and polarization in American politics.

The Baby Boomers, born between 1946 and 1964, have had a profound impact on America and the world. This generation experienced many historic events, including the civil rights movement, the Vietnam War, the rise of feminism, and the emergence of new technologies, which influenced their values and shaped their impact on society.

One of the most significant changes that the Baby Boomers brought to America was the rise of the counterculture movement in the 1960s. This movement challenged traditional social norms and values, including gender roles, sexual liberation, and civil rights. The Baby Boomers played a significant role in these movements, advocating for change and shaping the cultural landscape of the country.

Another significant impact of the Baby Boomers was their effect on the economy. As this generation began to enter the workforce in the 1970s and 1980s, they demanded higher wages and better working conditions, which led to a period of economic growth and prosperity. The Baby Boomers also had a significant impact on consumer behavior, as they became one of the largest generations of consumers in history.

In addition, the Baby Boomers also played a significant role in shaping politics and government policy. This generation was deeply divided on many issues, including the Vietnam War, civil rights, and feminism, which led to a highly charged political environment. The Baby Boomers were also influential in shaping government policies on issues such as healthcare, social security, and the environment.

The Baby Boomers also had a significant impact on technology, as they witnessed the emergence of personal computers, the internet, and social media. This generation embraced new technologies and was instrumental in their development and adoption, which transformed communication and information sharing.

In terms of their impact on family and relationships, the Baby Boomers were known for challenging traditional roles and norms. They were the first generation to embrace divorce and single parenthood, which led to significant changes in family dynamics and the social stigma associated with these issues.

Finally, the Baby Boomers also had a significant impact on the environment. As this generation became more politically active, they pushed for greater environmental protections and sustainability. This led to the creation of the Environmental Protection Agency and significant government action on issues such as air and water pollution, climate change, and wilderness preservation.

The Baby Boomers have had a profound impact on America and the world, shaping social, cultural, economic, political, technological, environmental, and family dynamics. Their influence will continue to be felt for generations to come, as they have shaped the course of history in countless ways.

The term "Baby Boomers" has also been adopted in other countries to describe their post-World War II generation. However, the impact of the Baby Boomers outside of America can vary greatly depending on the specific country and its history.

In countries that experienced a similar post-war demographic surge, such as Canada, Australia, and the United Kingdom, the Baby Boomer generation had a significant impact on society and culture. These countries also saw an increase in economic prosperity and consumerism during the 1960s and 1970s, as the Baby Boomers came of age and entered the workforce.

In Japan, the Baby Boomer generation is known as the "kohai sedai" (後輩世代), or "junior generation." This generation was heavily influenced by American culture and saw significant economic growth and modernization in Japan during the 1960s and 1970s.

In countries that did not experience a post-war baby boom, the impact of the Baby Boomer generation may be less pronounced. However, their influence can still be felt in global trends such as the rise of rock and roll music, the development of youth culture, and the push for social and political change.

It's difficult to pinpoint an exact date when other countries began to adopt the term "Baby Boomers," as it likely happened gradually over time as the demographic trend became more widely recognized. However, the term has been used in popular media and academic research around the world since at least the 1970s.

Overall, the Baby Boomer generation has had a significant impact on the world, both in America and beyond. Their sheer numbers and cultural influence have shaped everything from popular music and fashion to social and political movements. As this generation continues to age and enter retirement, their impact on society will likely continue to be felt for years to come.

The Baby Boomers represent a significant demographic shift in American society, with their idealism and commitment to personal growth shaping the counterculture movement and leading to significant social and cultural change.

However, their individualistic mindset has also contributed to a sense of entitlement and a lack of concern for the needs of the group. As they continue to age and retire, their impact on American society and politics will continue to be felt for years to come.

GENERATION X

The term "Generation X" was popularized by a book written by Douglas Coupland titled "Generation X: Tales for an Accelerated Culture," which was published in 1991. Coupland used the term to describe the generation of people born between the early 1960s and early 1980s, who were coming of age in a rapidly changing world. However, the term had been used previously by photographer Robert Capa in the early 1950s to describe young people in Europe who were living in the aftermath of World War II.

It wasn't until Coupland's book that the term became widely known and associated with the generation born in the 1960s and 1970s. "Generation X: Tales for an Accelerated Culture" is a novel by Canadian author Douglas Coupland, first published in 1991. The book is a series of loosely connected stories that follow the lives of three friends in their early twenties - Dag, Andy, and Claire - as they navigate through life in the late 1980s and early 1990s. The book explores themes of disillusionment, ennui, and disconnection, which were common experiences among young people at the time.

The book received mixed reviews upon its initial release, with some critics dismissing it as shallow and self-indulgent, while others praised it for its wit and insight into the culture of the time. However, over time, the book has come to be seen as a defining work of its era, and it is widely credited with popularizing the term "Generation X."

Since its release, the book has spawned a number of imitations and parodies, as well as a subgenre of fiction known as "slacker lit," which often focuses on the lives of disaffected young people.

Generation X is often referred to as the "forgotten" generation, as they came of age during a period of relative calm between two major events: the Vietnam War and the 9/11 terrorist attacks. This generation was born roughly between the mid-1960s and early 1980s, and they grew up in a time of economic uncertainty, political disillusionment, and social change.

During the 1970s and 1980s, America experienced a shift away from traditional values and social structures. This was the era of the civil rights movement, the sexual revolution, and the feminist movement, and it had a profound impact on Generation X. Many of them grew up in broken homes, with divorced or single parents, and they were often left to fend for themselves.

The economic conditions of the time were also challenging, with high inflation and unemployment rates. Many Gen Xers entered the workforce during a time of recession, which made it difficult for them to establish themselves in stable careers. This led to a sense of independence and self-reliance, as they were forced to find creative ways to support themselves.

One defining characteristic of Generation X is their skepticism and mistrust of institutions, including the government, corporations, and the media. This is partly due to the disillusionment that came out of Watergate and other political scandals of the time, as well as the rise of consumerism and the sense that society had become too focused on material possessions.

Despite these challenges, Generation X also showed a strong entrepreneurial spirit, with many of them starting their own businesses or pursuing non-traditional career paths. This was partly due to the influence of the Silicon Valley tech boom, which provided new opportunities for innovation and disruption.

In terms of family and relationships, Generation X is often seen as more independent and less traditional than previous generations. They are more likely to delay marriage and child-rearing, and they place a high value on work-life balance and personal fulfillment.

Overall, Generation X is a complex and multifaceted generation, shaped by the social, economic, and political forces of their time. Their attitudes toward work, family, and politics reflect their experiences of growing up in a period of great change and uncertainty, and they will continue to shape America's future in unique and unexpected ways.

Generation X, had a significant impact on American society. Here are some of the ways in which they contributed to social and cultural evolution:

Technological advancements: Generation X was the first generation to grow up with personal computers and the internet. They played a significant role in driving the technological revolution of the 1980s and 1990s, which transformed communication, commerce, and entertainment.

Alternative culture: Gen Xers embraced alternative music, fashion, and lifestyles that challenged mainstream norms. They were associated with the rise of punk, grunge, and hip-hop music, as well as the popularity of independent films, graphic novels, and comic books.

Entrepreneurial spirit: Generation X grew up during an era of economic uncertainty and witnessed the decline of traditional industries. As a result, many members of this generation developed an entrepreneurial spirit and sought to create their own businesses or pursue freelance careers.

Diversity and inclusion: Gen Xers were the first generation to grow up in a more diverse and inclusive society. They were exposed to a wider range of cultures, religions, and lifestyles, which influenced their values and beliefs. They were also more likely to support progressive causes such as gay rights, racial equality, and environmentalism.

Work-life balance: Generation X was the first generation to prioritize work-life balance, seeking careers that allowed them to pursue personal interests and spend time with their families. They also pushed for greater flexibility in the workplace, such as telecommuting and job-sharing.

Political activism: Gen Xers were known for their skepticism and cynicism toward traditional political institutions. However, they also played a significant role in political activism, particularly in the areas of environmentalism and human rights.

Generation X contributed to the evolution of American society by embracing technological advancements, challenging traditional norms, promoting diversity and inclusion, prioritizing work-life balance, and engaging in political activism. Their impact continues to shape the cultural and social landscape of the United States.

The term "Generation X" originated in the United States, but its influence has spread beyond American borders. The impact of this generation has been felt in various areas, including culture, business, politics, and technology.

In terms of culture, Generation X played a significant role in shaping popular music, fashion, and film during the 1980s and 1990s. This generation embraced a DIY (do-it-yourself) ethos and a sense of individualism, which was reflected in the rise of alternative music, grunge fashion, and independent cinema. Generation X also grew up with the emergence of video games, which has since become a global industry.

In business, Generation X was the first to be raised in a digital age, and many members of this generation were early adopters of new technologies such as personal computers and the internet. This digital fluency has given Gen Xers an advantage in the modern workplace, where technology plays an increasingly important role.

Politically, Generation X came of age during a time of political conservatism in the United States, and many members of this generation developed a healthy skepticism toward authority and traditional institutions. This skepticism has influenced political discourse in the U.S. and beyond, leading to a focus on individualism, self-reliance, and entrepreneurship.

Outside of the U.S., Generation X has had a significant impact in countries such as Canada, Australia, and the United Kingdom. In Canada, Gen Xers have had a notable impact on the arts and entertainment industries, while in Australia, they have been credited with revitalizing the economy through their entrepreneurial spirit. In the UK, Gen Xers have played a key role in shaping political discourse and social values.

The impact of Generation X has been felt around the world, particularly in areas such as technology, business, and culture. While this generation may not have received the same level of attention as Baby Boomers or Millennials, their contributions have been significant and continue to shape the world we live in today.

"The Cultural Contradictions That Have Crippled Gen X" is an article written by Paul Taylor and published in The Atlantic in 2014. In the article, Taylor argues that Generation X has faced unique challenges and cultural contradictions that have had a significant impact on their lives and careers.

Taylor points out that Generation X is often overlooked or dismissed as a "lost" generation, caught between the Baby Boomers and Millennials. He notes that Gen Xers grew up in a time of economic upheaval and societal change, which led to a sense of cynicism and skepticism about institutions and authority. This skepticism, coupled with a desire for authenticity and autonomy, has made it difficult for Gen Xers to find a place in a society that often values conformity and obedience.

Taylor also discusses the impact of technology on Gen X, noting that while they are digital natives, they are also the last generation to remember life before the internet. This has created a tension between the desire for connection and the need for privacy and autonomy. Overall, the article argues that the cultural contradictions that have shaped Gen X have had a profound impact on their lives and will continue to shape their futures.

There are many great articles and books that talk about Generation X.
Here are a few examples:

"Generation X: Tales for an Accelerated Culture" by Douglas Coupland - This novel is often credited with popularizing the term "Generation X" and portrays the experiences of a group of young adults struggling to find their place in the world.

"The Defining Decade: Why Your Twenties Matter--And How to Make the Most of Them Now" by Meg Jay - This book explores the challenges that face young adults in their 20s and offers practical advice for navigating this stage of life. It also touches on the specific experiences of the Generation X cohort.

"Generation X Goes Global: Mapping a Youth Culture in Motion" edited by Christine Henseler - This book examines the ways in which Generation X has influenced global culture and features essays from scholars and cultural critics from around the world.

"Generation X: Americans Born 1965 to 1976" by Paul Taylor - This report from the Pew Research Center provides statistical data and analysis of the Generation X cohort, including their political and social attitudes, economic situation, and family dynamics.

"The Gen Xperience: Growing Up and Living in the Shadow of the Boom" edited by Jen Abbas - This anthology features personal essays from members of the Generation X cohort and explores the ways in which their experiences have been shaped by their unique historical and cultural context.

"Generation X Rocks: Contemporary Peninsular Fiction, Film, and Rock Culture" by Ivy A. Corfis - This book examines the influence of rock music on Generation X and its impact on contemporary Spanish and Latin American literature and film.

"The Last Days of Disco: Why the 70s Still Matter" by James Wolcott - This essay reflects on the cultural legacy of the Baby Boomers and the influence of their cultural artifacts on Generation X and subsequent generations.

Barack Obama: Born in 1961, Obama served as the 44th President of the United States from 2009 to 2017. He is the first African American to hold the presidency and is credited with introducing several policies that have had a significant impact on America and the world, including the Affordable Care Act (Obamacare), the Dodd-Frank Wall Street Reform and Consumer Protection Act, and the Paris Agreement on climate change.

Elon Musk: Born in 1971, Musk is a business magnate, inventor, and engineer. He is the founder and CEO of SpaceX, Tesla, Neuralink, and The Boring Company. He is known for his innovative ideas in the fields of space exploration, renewable energy, and transportation.

Jeff Bezos: Born in 1964, Bezos is the founder and CEO of Amazon, which is one of the world's largest online retailers. He has played a significant role in the growth of e-commerce and has revolutionized the retail industry with his company's innovative business model.

Serena Williams: Born in 1981, Williams is a professional tennis player who has won 23 Grand Slam singles titles, making her the most successful player in the Open Era. She has also been an advocate for women's rights and has spoken out about issues such as pay inequality in sports.

Lin-Manuel Miranda: Born in 1980, Miranda is a composer, lyricist, actor, and playwright. He is best known for creating the hit musicals Hamilton and In the Heights. He has been recognized for his contributions to theater and has won several awards, including the Pulitzer Prize for Drama.

Sheryl Sandberg: Born in 1969, Sandberg is a business executive and author. She is the chief operating officer (COO) of Facebook and has been a vocal advocate for gender equality in the workplace. She has also authored several books, including Lean In: Women, Work, and the Will to Lead.

Ai Weiwei - Born in China, Ai Weiwei is a contemporary artist and activist who is known for his social and political commentary in his works. He has used his art to address issues such as government corruption and human rights violations.

David Beckham - Born in England, Beckham is a former professional footballer who has had a significant impact on the sport both on and off the field. He is considered one of the greatest players of his generation and has also been involved in numerous philanthropic and business ventures.

Angela Merkel - Born in Germany, Merkel is a politician who served as the Chancellor of Germany from 2005 to 2021. She is known for her leadership during the European debt crisis and the Syrian refugee crisis, as well as her commitment to climate change and renewable energy.

Jacinda Ardern (1980-) - the Prime Minister of New Zealand since 2017, Ardern is the youngest female leader in the world and has gained international attention for her compassionate and progressive leadership style. Under her leadership, New Zealand has implemented several significant policies, such as banning assault weapons and providing free menstrual products in schools.

Emmanuel Macron (1977-) - the current President of France, Macron has been instrumental in reforming the French economy and political system. He has also been a prominent voice in promoting European unity and combating climate change.

Banksy (born 1974) - English street artist and political activist whose identity remains unknown. Banksy's artwork often contains social commentary and critiques of capitalism, consumerism, and war. His works have been exhibited around the world and sold for millions of dollars.

MILLENIALS OR GENERATION Y

As I said before, the term "Millennials" was coined by authors William Strauss and Neil Howe in their 1991 book "Generations: The History of America's Future, 1584 to 2069." The book explores the cyclical patterns of generational attitudes and behaviors in American history.

Strauss and Howe used the term "Millennials" to describe the generation born between 1982 and 2004, who would come of age around the turn of the millennium. The term references the new millennium and the significant cultural, social, and technological changes that this generation would experience.

The authors noted that the Millennials were shaped by the cultural shifts of the 1990s, including the rise of the internet and globalization. They also described the Millennials as a highly diverse generation, with a strong focus on community, collaboration, and social justice.

Since the publication of "Generations," the term "Millennials" has become widely used in popular culture and academia to describe this cohort of young people.

The Millennials, also known as Generation Y, were born between 1981 and 1996. They came of age during a time of rapid technological change, economic turbulence, and global interconnectedness. Many Millennials were raised by Baby Boomer parents who instilled in them a sense of optimism, self-esteem, and a desire for personal fulfillment.

Millennials are the most diverse generation in American history, with a higher proportion of minorities and foreign-born individuals than any previous generation. They are also the most educated generation, with more of them attending college than any other cohort. This has led to a greater emphasis on knowledge work, entrepreneurship, and innovation, as Millennials seek to create their own paths and define success on their own terms.

At the same time, Millennials face significant challenges, including mounting student debt, limited job opportunities, and increasing income inequality. They also came of age during a time of global instability, marked by terrorist attacks, natural disasters, and the Great Recession of 2008.

Despite these challenges, Millennials have shown a strong commitment to social justice, environmental sustainability, and community involvement. They are more likely than previous generations to volunteer, donate to charity, and engage in political activism. They are also known for their digital fluency, social media savvy, and preference for mobile technology.

In terms of work, Millennials prioritize flexibility, work-life balance, and meaningful work over traditional measures of success such as salary and status. They value collaboration and feedback, and tend to work well in teams. They are also more likely to job-hop than previous generations, as they seek to find the right fit and pursue their passions.

In terms of family, Millennials are delaying marriage and child-rearing, and are more likely to live with their parents or roommates than previous generations. This is partly due to financial constraints, but also reflects a desire for independence and exploration. They are also more likely to prioritize gender and LGBTQ+ equality, and to support policies that support work-life balance and family leave.

Overall, Millennials are a generation marked by their idealism, diversity, and adaptability. They face significant challenges, but also hold great promise for shaping the future of America and the world.

Here are some potential impacts of the Millennial generation in each of those areas:

A. Work: The Millennial generation has placed a strong emphasis on work-life balance, flexibility, and meaningful work. They have also been known for job hopping more frequently than previous generations, seeking out opportunities that align with their values and offer personal growth.

B. Mindset: Millennials have been characterized as optimistic, confident, and collaborative. They have grown up with technology and tend to be comfortable with change and innovation. They are also more likely to prioritize social and environmental issues.

C. Life Expectations: Millennials have faced economic challenges such as high levels of student debt and a difficult job market, leading to delayed milestones such as marriage and homeownership. However, they are generally optimistic about their future and see the potential for positive change in the world.

D. Traveling: Millennials have been known for valuing experiences over material possessions, and travel has been a key part of that. They are more likely to seek out unique and authentic experiences, and prioritize sustainability and cultural immersion in their travel choices.

E. Medicine: As the first generation to grow up with widespread access to the internet, Millennials have been proactive in seeking out health information and resources online. They have also been more likely to prioritize mental health and wellness, and to seek out alternative medicine and holistic approaches to healthcare.

There are many important articles that discuss the Millennial or Gen Y generation.

Here are a few examples:

"Millennials: The Me Me Me Generation" by Joel Stein, published in Time magazine in 2013. This article explores the stereotype of Millennials as entitled and self-absorbed, and examines how their upbringing and the changing cultural landscape have contributed to this perception.

"The Overprotected Kid" by Hanna Rosin, published in The Atlantic in 2014. This article looks at how Millennial parents' tendency to shelter and micromanage their children has led to a decline in free play and exploration, and how this may be negatively impacting children's development.

"Why Millennials Keep Dumping You: An Open Letter to Management" by Rachel Bitte, published in Forbes in 2016. This article offers advice to employers on how to attract and retain Millennial employees, including providing opportunities for growth and flexibility, and creating a company culture that aligns with Millennial values.

"The Burnout Generation" by Anne Helen Petersen, published in Buzzfeed News in 2019. This article examines the phenomenon of Millennial burnout, exploring how societal and economic factors have contributed to this pervasive feeling of exhaustion and disillusionment among young adults.

"The Myth of the Millennial Entrepreneur" by Mark L. Rockefeller, published in Entrepreneur in 2021. This article challenges the popular narrative of Millennials as a generation of entrepreneurs, arguing that the reality is more nuanced and that systemic barriers may be preventing many young people from starting their own businesses.

Mark Zuckerberg (1984) - Co-founder and CEO of Facebook, a platform that has revolutionized social networking and online communication.

Kylie Jenner (1997) - American reality TV personality, entrepreneur, and founder of Kylie Cosmetics. She became the youngest self-made billionaire in history in 2019 at the age of 21.

Simone Biles (1997) - American gymnast who has won 30 Olympic and World Championship medals, making her the most decorated gymnast of all time.

Emma Watson (1990) - British actress and activist, best known for her role as Hermione Granger in the Harry Potter film series. She is also a UN Women Goodwill Ambassador and a strong advocate for women's rights.

Malala Yousafzai (1997) - Pakistani activist for female education and the youngest Nobel Prize laureate. She survived a Taliban assassination attempt and has since become a global advocate for girls' education.

Chance the Rapper (1993) - American rapper, singer, and songwriter who has won multiple Grammy Awards and is known for his philanthropic efforts in his hometown of Chicago.

Rihanna (1988) - Barbadian singer, songwriter, actress, and businesswoman. She is one of the best-selling music artists of all time and has also been recognized for her humanitarian work.

Justin Bieber (1994) - Canadian singer, songwriter, and actor who gained popularity through his YouTube videos and has since become one of the best-selling music artists of all time.

Greta Thunberg (2003) - Swedish environmental activist who gained international attention for her school strike for climate movement and her outspoken criticism of world leaders' inaction on climate change.

Michael B. Jordan (1987) - American actor and producer who has starred in several critically acclaimed films, including Black Panther and Creed, and has been recognized for his advocacy for diversity and representation in Hollywood.

THE GENERATION Z

Even the term "Generation Z" was first coined by Strauss and Howe in their book "Generations: The History of America's Future, 1584 to 2069" in 1991. However, it was not widely used until the early 2010s when the generation began to come of age.

Generation Z is defined as those born between 1997 and 2012, and they are currently the youngest generation in society. They are sometimes referred to as "digital natives" due to their exposure to technology from a very young age, particularly smartphones and social media.

Generation Z has grown up in a world shaped by events such as the global financial crisis, climate change, and the rise of social media. They are often characterized as being socially conscious and highly focused on issues such as diversity, equality, and sustainability. They have been shaped by their exposure to a wide range of global issues through social media, and are highly motivated to make a positive impact on the world. This activism is evident in the various social movements led by young people, such as the March for Our Lives movement against gun violence in schools, and the global youth-led climate strikes.

Generation Z is also highly entrepreneurial, and many are looking to start their own businesses or create social enterprises that align with their values. They are highly creative, often using technology to create and share their own content, and they are comfortable with the gig economy and freelance work.

In terms of their education and career aspirations, Generation Z tends to be highly focused on practical skills and real-world experience. They value education and personal development, but are also interested in finding ways to gain experience and build their resumes outside of traditional educational pathways. Many are interested in pursuing careers in technology, healthcare, and social impact sectors.

As the oldest members of Generation Z are just entering adulthood, their impact on the world is still unfolding. However, there are already some notable trends and areas of impact that can be observed.

Economically, Generation Z is marked by their relationship with technology and digital media. They are the first generation to have grown up with smartphones and social media as ubiquitous parts of their lives. As such, they are highly connected and tend to be adept at using technology to solve problems and find information. This has led to the rise of new industries and business models, such as influencer marketing and e-commerce.

In terms of the environment, Generation Z is marked by their concerns about climate change and sustainability. Growing up in an era of increasing awareness about the impacts of human activity on the planet, they are more likely than previous generations to prioritize environmental responsibility and advocate for action on climate change. This has already led to the rise of new industries, such as clean energy and sustainable products.

In the arts, Generation Z is characterized by their diversity and their embrace of new forms of expression. They are more likely than previous generations to reject traditional labels and boundaries, such as those between different art forms or between high and low culture. This has led to the rise of new genres and art movements, such as meme culture and digital art. Additionally, Generation Z is more likely to engage with art and culture through social media and other digital platforms, which has created new opportunities and challenges for artists and creators.

"Generation Z Is Making Waves in Social Activism" by Forbes: This article discusses how Gen Z is using their social media prowess and digital nativism to advocate for social justice causes and create change in their communities.

"Generation Z and the Future of Work" by Deloitte: This article explores how Gen Z's unique perspectives and skills will shape the future of work, including their preference for a diverse and inclusive workplace, their desire for work-life balance, and their ability to adapt to new technology.

"Generation Z: A Look at the Technology and Media Habits of Today's Teens" by Pew Research Center: This report delves into the media and technology habits of Gen Z, including their social media use, smartphone ownership, and online activities.

"Generation Z Wants to Save the World. Can We Let Them?" by The New York Times: This opinion piece discusses how Gen Z's passion for social justice and environmentalism is inspiring, but also raises questions about whether previous generations have done enough to address these issues.

"Generation Z and the Future of Retail" by Retail Dive: This article explores how Gen Z's shopping habits and preferences are disrupting the retail industry, including their preference for online shopping and demand for sustainability and ethical business practices.

"The Economic Reality of Generation Z" by The Wall Street Journal: This article discusses the economic challenges facing Gen Z, including the high cost of education, limited job opportunities, and rising cost of living.

"Why Generation Z Is Turning to TikTok for Financial Advice" by CNBC: This article explores how Gen Z is using social media, particularly TikTok, to learn about personal finance and investing.

"Generation Z is driving the future of wellness" by Vogue Business: This article explores how Gen Z is shaping the wellness industry, including their focus on mental health, sustainability, and holistic well-being.

"The Future is Diverse: How Gen Z is Pushing the Advertising Industry Forward" by Adweek: This article discusses how Gen Z's demand for diversity and inclusion is driving changes in the advertising industry, including the need for more diverse representation in advertising campaigns.

"Meet Gen Z: How to Connect with the Newest Generation of Homebuyers" by Realtor Magazine: This article explores how Gen Z's homebuying habits and preferences are different from previous generations, including their desire for eco-friendly homes, smart home technology, and online homebuying experiences.

THE GENERATION ALPHA

Generation Alpha is a term that has gained traction in recent years to describe the cohort born after 2012. While it may not have been widely mentioned by a specific individual, the term has emerged organically as a way to distinguish this new generation from previous ones. As the children of millennials and the first generation born entirely in the 21st century, Generation Alpha is expected to be shaped by unique circumstances and experiences.

One defining characteristic of Generation Alpha is their relationship with technology. From the moment they are born, they are surrounded by smartphones, tablets, and other digital devices. Technology is an integral part of their lives, and they navigate digital platforms with ease. This constant exposure to technology has significant implications for their behavior, cognitive development, and future prospects.

In terms of education, Generation Alpha is likely to experience a shift in learning methodologies.

Traditional classrooms are being transformed by digital tools and personalized learning approaches. The use of educational apps, online resources, and interactive platforms will provide new opportunities for tailored learning experiences. Technology will play a vital role in preparing Generation Alpha for the rapidly evolving job market, where digital skills and adaptability will be highly valued.

The influence of technology on social interactions is another key aspect of Generation Alpha's development. Growing up with social media, they will have a different perspective on communication and relationships. Online platforms offer them unprecedented connectivity and the ability to engage with diverse communities globally. However, there will also be challenges, such as concerns about privacy, cyberbullying, and the impact of social media on mental health. Society will need to navigate these issues and provide guidance to ensure a healthy balance between virtual and real-world connections.

As Generation Alpha reaches adulthood, they will enter a world shaped by rapid technological advancements. Automation, artificial intelligence, and other emerging technologies will continue to transform industries and redefine job requirements. This generation will need to be adaptable and possess a strong foundation in digital literacy to succeed in this changing landscape. New professions and industries will arise, presenting both opportunities and challenges.

The future of Generation Alpha extends beyond America's borders. As a global generation connected through digital platforms, they will have a unique perspective on global issues and a sense of global citizenship. They are likely to be passionate about social justice, sustainability, and making a positive impact on the world. With their global mindset and access to information, Generation Alpha has the potential to drive significant change on a global scale. However, it is important to consider that the future is not predetermined, and the path of Generation Alpha will be influenced by numerous factors. Economic, political, and environmental circumstances will shape their opportunities and challenges. Additionally, the role of parents, educators, and policymakers in nurturing their potential and providing a supportive environment will be crucial.

In conclusion, Generation Alpha represents a new era shaped by technology and connectivity. Their lives will be marked by digital experiences, online relationships, and a global outlook. As they navigate the challenges and opportunities of the future, their ability to adapt, innovate, and positively influence society will play a vital role in shaping the world for generations to come.

Gen Alpha signifies their status as the first generation to be born entirely in the 21st century and is growing up in a highly digital and technologically advanced world. They are exposed to technology from a very young age, with smartphones, tablets, and the internet being integral parts of their lives. This constant exposure to technology has shaped their behavior and interaction with the world around them.

Generation Alpha is expected to be highly tech-savvy, comfortable with digital platforms, and quick to adapt to new technologies.

They are likely to have a deep understanding of social media, digital communication, and online content consumption. This generation may also experience changes in the job market, with emerging careers that are heavily influenced by technology, such as artificial intelligence, virtual reality, and automation.

The impact of technology on Generation Alpha's behavior and development is a topic of ongoing study and speculation.

Researchers and experts are closely observing how this constant exposure to technology may shape their cognitive abilities, social skills, and overall well-being. As this generation continues to grow and mature, their unique characteristics and contributions to society will become more apparent.

GENERATIONS IN EUROPE, ESPECIALLY IN ITALY AND UK

The impact of generations extends beyond the borders of the United States and has had significant effects on Europe as well, including countries like Italy and the United Kingdom. Let's delve into the influence of each generation, starting with the Silent Generation.

The Silent Generation, born between 1928 and 1945, experienced the aftermath of World War II and witnessed Europe's efforts to rebuild and recover. In Italy, this generation played a crucial role in the country's post-war reconstruction, contributing to the economic boom known as the "Italian Miracle." With their strong work ethic and resilience, the Silent Generation laid the foundation for Italy's economic growth, emphasizing stability, family values, and community cohesion.

Similarly, in the United Kingdom, the Silent Generation contributed to the country's post-war recovery and the reconstruction of its infrastructure.

They experienced the hardships of rationing and the challenges of rebuilding a nation devastated by war. Their commitment to hard work and traditional values, combined with the establishment of welfare systems, set the stage for the country's future development.

Moving on to the Baby Boomers, born between 1946 and 1964, this generation played a pivotal role in shaping Europe's social and cultural landscape. In Italy, the Baby Boomers witnessed a period of profound social change, challenging traditional norms and advocating for civil rights and individual freedoms. They participated in student movements and protested against social injustices, leaving a lasting impact on Italian society.

Similarly, in the United Kingdom, the Baby Boomers brought about cultural revolutions and transformative movements. They challenged societal norms, driving progressive changes in areas such as women's rights, LGBTQ+ rights, and anti-racism. Their activism, combined with their economic influence, shaped the social fabric of the country and laid the groundwork for future advancements.

Generation X, born between 1965 and 1980, witnessed a time of economic and political transition in both Italy and the United Kingdom. In Italy, this generation experienced economic downturns, political corruption scandals, and a shifting job market. They adapted to these challenges, embracing entrepreneurship and innovation, and became drivers of economic growth and technological advancements.

In the United Kingdom, Generation X played a crucial role in the country's transition from traditional industries to a more service-oriented economy. They embraced globalization, fostering international connections and contributing to the growth of the financial sector. This generation also witnessed the rise of the European Union and the impact of European integration on the country's politics and economy.

Moving to the Millennial generation, born between 1981 and 1996, their impact on Europe, including Italy and the United Kingdom, has been shaped by technological advancements and globalization. In Italy, Millennials have been at the forefront of social change, advocating for sustainability, social justice, and inclusivity. They have embraced digital technology and social media as tools for activism and have pushed for political and cultural reforms.

Similarly, in the United Kingdom, Millennials have been instrumental in driving innovation and embracing the digital age. They have played a crucial role in the growth of the creative industries and the development of technology startups. Their values, such as environmental consciousness and diversity, have influenced consumer trends and business practices.

As for Generation Z, born between 1997 and 2012, their impact is still unfolding, but early signs suggest a generation deeply engaged in social issues, technology, and global interconnectedness. In both Italy and the United Kingdom, Gen Z individuals have been at the forefront of movements addressing climate change, equality, and social justice. They are leveraging social media and digital platforms to amplify their voices and demand change.

In conclusion, each generation has left its mark on Europe, including Italy and the United Kingdom, through their unique experiences, values, and contributions. From the Silent Generation's rebuilding efforts to the transformative activism of the Baby Boomers, the entrepreneurial spirit of Generation X, the digital advancements of the Millennials, and the socially conscious activism of Generation Z, the impact of generations in Europe has been profound and far-reaching.

In Italy, the intergenerational dynamics have influenced societal values and cultural norms. The Silent Generation's emphasis on family and community cohesion continues to shape Italian society, with strong family bonds and traditions playing a significant role in daily life. The Baby Boomers' activism and pursuit of individual freedoms have challenged traditional structures and contributed to a more progressive and inclusive society. Generation X's entrepreneurial spirit and adaptability have helped navigate economic challenges and fostered innovation and technological advancements. Meanwhile, Millennials and Generation Z are pushing for environmental sustainability, social equality, and digital transformation, leveraging their voices and digital fluency to bring about positive change.

Similarly, in the United Kingdom, the impact of generations is evident in various aspects of society. The Silent Generation's resilience and commitment to rebuilding after World War II laid the foundation for the country's economic recovery. The Baby Boomers' activism and cultural revolutions have brought about significant social changes, promoting equality and diversity. Generation X's embrace of globalization and technological advancements has driven economic growth and transformed industries. Millennials and Generation Z are challenging traditional power structures, advocating for environmental sustainability, and leveraging digital platforms to connect and mobilize for social causes.

The interplay between generations is particularly notable in the realms of politics, economics, and cultural expressions. Political landscapes in both countries have been shaped by the values and aspirations of different generations, influencing policy decisions, voter demographics, and social movements. Economically, each generation has contributed to the growth and evolution of industries, adapting to changing market trends and technological advancements. Furthermore, cultural expressions, including art, music, fashion, and literature, have been influenced by generational perspectives, reflecting the shifting social dynamics and values of each era.

Looking to the future, the impact of generations will continue to shape Europe, Italy, and the United Kingdom in profound ways. As Generation Z comes of age and takes on more prominent roles in society, their digital nativism, focus on social justice, and global interconnectedness will drive further social, economic, and environmental transformations. The challenges and opportunities presented by technological advancements, climate change, and societal issues will require collaborative efforts across generations to create sustainable and inclusive societies.

In conclusion, generations in Europe, including Italy and the United Kingdom, have left an indelible mark on society, influencing cultural norms, driving social progress, and shaping economic landscapes. By understanding and appreciating the contributions and perspectives of each generation, we can foster greater intergenerational understanding, bridge gaps, and collectively navigate the challenges and possibilities of the future.

.

GENERATIONS IN ASIA, ESPECIALLY IN JAPAN

In Asia, the impact of generations, including in Japan, has been instrumental in shaping the social, economic, and cultural landscape of the region. Each generation brings unique experiences, values, and perspectives that have influenced the trajectory of Japan's development and its place in the global arena.

Starting with the Silent Generation, which experienced the tumultuous period of World War II and the subsequent post-war reconstruction, their resilience and dedication to rebuilding the nation laid the foundation for Japan's rapid economic growth. Their hard work, discipline, and commitment to collective progress became ingrained in the Japanese society and contributed to its transformation into an economic powerhouse.

The Baby Boomers in Japan witnessed a period of unprecedented economic prosperity during the post-war era. They played a pivotal role in shaping Japan's industrial expansion and technological advancements. The Baby Boomers embraced modernization, consumerism, and an aspiration for higher living standards. This generation witnessed the emergence of Japan as a global economic leader and the subsequent challenges of economic downturns, leading to a reevaluation of societal priorities.

Generation X in Japan experienced a period of economic stagnation and increasing globalization. They adapted to the changing economic landscape, embracing new technologies and exploring alternative career paths. Generation X in Japan witnessed the bursting of the economic bubble in the 1990s, which led to a shift in societal values and a reexamination of traditional norms. Their resilience, adaptability, and entrepreneurial spirit played a crucial role in rebuilding Japan's economy and fostering innovation.

The Millennial generation in Japan grew up in an increasingly interconnected and digital world. They witnessed the impact of globalization, technological advancements, and environmental challenges. Millennials in Japan are known for their pursuit of work-life balance, emphasis on personal fulfillment, and social consciousness. They are pushing for societal change, advocating for diversity, sustainability, and inclusivity. The Millennials' digital fluency and global outlook have influenced Japan's business practices, communication patterns, and cultural expressions.

Generation Z, the current and youngest generation in Japan, has been shaped by a highly connected and technologically driven society. They are digital natives who have grown up with smartphones, social media, and instant access to information. Generation Z in

Japan is characterized by their entrepreneurial spirit, diverse perspectives, and commitment to social causes. They prioritize individuality, creativity, and environmental sustainability. This generation is poised to lead Japan into the future, leveraging technology and global connections to address pressing challenges and reshape traditional systems.

In addition to the economic impact, generations in Japan have also influenced cultural expressions, social values, and political dynamics. From literature and art to fashion and music, each generation has contributed to Japan's rich cultural tapestry. Socially, generational shifts have brought changes in family structures, gender roles, and social norms. Politically, different generations have influenced electoral outcomes, policy priorities, and civic engagement.

Looking ahead, the impact of generations in Japan will continue to shape the nation's future. The challenges of an aging population, technological advancements, and global uncertainties will require collaboration and innovative solutions across generations. Embracing the strengths and perspectives of each generation and fostering intergenerational dialogue will be vital in navigating the complexities and opportunities of the changing world.

In the realm of business and innovation, generations in Japan have contributed significantly to technological advancements and entrepreneurial endeavors. The Silent Generation, with their work ethic and dedication to rebuilding the nation, laid the groundwork for Japan's manufacturing prowess. Baby

Boomers, driven by economic growth, led Japan's technological advancements, particularly in the fields of electronics and automotive industries. Their contributions elevated Japan as a global leader in innovation.

Generation X in Japan, faced with economic challenges, embraced entrepreneurship and introduced new business models. They played a pivotal role in the development of Japan's tech startup scene, fostering a culture of risk-taking and creativity. This generation's emphasis on individuality and self-expression brought forth unique products and services that resonated with both domestic and international markets.

The Millennial generation in Japan has further expanded the entrepreneurial landscape. They have leveraged digital platforms and social media to launch innovative startups, disrupting traditional industries and introducing new business paradigms. With their global mindset and willingness to embrace technology, Millennials in Japan have cultivated a vibrant startup ecosystem, contributing to job creation, economic growth, and technological advancements.

In the environmental realm, generations in Japan have recognized the urgency of addressing sustainability challenges. The Silent Generation witnessed the devastating aftermath of World War II and embraced the importance of conservation and resource management. Their values of frugality and minimal waste laid the foundation for Japan's commitment to environmental stewardship.

Baby Boomers in Japan witnessed the negative environmental impacts of rapid industrialization and became advocates for environmental protection. They contributed to the establishment of environmental regulations and initiatives, paving the way for greater environmental consciousness.

Generation X in Japan furthered the sustainability agenda by emphasizing renewable energy sources, waste reduction, and eco-friendly practices. They pushed for corporate responsibility and environmentally conscious business practices, promoting a greener economy.

Millennials in Japan have taken up the mantle of environmental activism. They are actively engaged in advocating for climate action, sustainable consumption, and environmental justice. With their digital fluency and ability to mobilize social movements, Millennials have raised awareness on pressing environmental issues and influenced policy discussions.

In the realm of arts and culture, generations in Japan have brought forth unique expressions, blending tradition with modernity. The Silent Generation witnessed a revival of traditional arts, such as kabuki and Noh theater, preserving Japan's cultural heritage.

Baby Boomers in Japan embraced pop culture, including manga, anime, and J-pop, which gained global popularity. Their creative contributions influenced global entertainment industries and helped shape Japan's soft power.

Generation X in Japan witnessed a fusion of traditional and modern art forms. They explored diverse artistic expressions, pushing boundaries and challenging societal norms. Their contributions enriched Japan's contemporary art scene, attracting international acclaim.

Millennials in Japan have embraced new forms of artistic expression, leveraging digital platforms to showcase their creativity. From online art communities to virtual reality experiences,
Millennials in Japan have redefined the boundaries of art, reflecting their digital upbringing and global perspectives.

We can say that 'Generations' in Japan have made significant contributions to various aspects of society, including business, innovation, environmental sustainability, and arts and culture. Each generation has built upon the achievements of their predecessors, leaving their own unique imprint on Japan's development.
By recognizing the strengths and perspectives of each generation and fostering intergenerational collaboration, Japan can harness the collective power of its diverse population to tackle future challenges and seize opportunities for growth and progress.

In conclusion, generations in Japan have played a crucial role in shaping the country's social, economic, and cultural landscape. From the Silent Generation's post-war reconstruction efforts to the Baby Boomers' economic prosperity, Generation X's adaptability, the Millennials' pursuit of social change, and Generation Z's technological fluency, each generation has left an indelible mark on Japan's development.

By recognizing and harnessing the strengths and contributions of each generation, Japan can navigate the future with resilience, innovation, and unity.

GENERATIONS IN AFRICA

In the vast and diverse continent of Africa, each generation has left its mark on history, contributing to the shaping of nations, economies, and societies. From the Silent Generation to Millennials, their actions have had profound impacts on the continent's development, addressing challenges and paving the way for progress.

The Silent Generation in Africa emerged during a time of colonial rule and witnessed the struggle for independence. Their determination and resilience played a crucial role in liberating nations and establishing self-governance. These individuals became pioneers of change, shaping political landscapes and advocating for socioeconomic development. Despite facing economic limitations and dependence on cash crops, some members of the Silent Generation initiated industrial projects, promoted education, and built infrastructure that became the foundation for future growth.

Following the Silent Generation, the Baby Boomers in Africa experienced a period of post-independence nation-building. This generation actively participated in shaping the continent's development. While economic challenges such as external debt and political instability persisted, Baby Boomers contributed to various sectors, including entrepreneurship, finance, technology, and infrastructure development. Their efforts drove economic growth and created opportunities for progress.

As the continent continued to evolve, Generation X emerged as a transformative force in Africa. This generation witnessed political and economic transitions, advocating for democratic reforms, human rights, and social justice. In response to challenges such as corruption and inequality, Generation X played a vital role in promoting good governance and driving socio-economic transformation. Their entrepreneurial spirit and leadership resulted in the growth of private sectors, attracting foreign investments, and fostering technological advancements.

Today, the Millennial generation in Africa is characterized by its optimism, digital fluency, and social activism. This generation has harnessed the power of technology and social media to amplify their voices, advocate for change, and address pressing issues such as climate change and gender equality. Millennial entrepreneurs have emerged, leading innovation and contributing to economic growth through start-ups and disruptive technologies.

In Africa, the impact of these generations goes beyond economic and industrial growth. Their actions have shaped social dynamics, challenged existing norms, and paved the way for greater inclusivity. From grassroots movements to political leadership, these generations have strived to create more equitable societies, uplifting the marginalized and empowering the youth.

While each generation has faced unique challenges and opportunities, their collective efforts have driven progress in Africa. From the fight for independence to the pursuit of sustainable development, these generations have left indelible imprints on the continent's history. As the journey continues, the lessons learned from the past can guide the future, ensuring a more prosperous and inclusive Africa for generations to come.

Throughout Africa's history, several significant events and historical facts have shaped the experiences and perspectives of different generations, influencing their actions and contributions to society. Here are some key historical facts that have had a profound impact on African generations:

Colonialism: The era of colonial rule, which lasted from the late 19th century to the mid-20th century, greatly influenced the Silent Generation in Africa. Colonial powers imposed political, economic, and social structures that shaped the region's trajectory.

The struggle for independence against colonial rule became a defining moment, leading to the emergence of leaders and activists who fought for self-determination and laid the foundation for post-colonial nations.

Independence Movements: The mid-20th century saw a wave of independence movements sweep across Africa. Influential leaders such as Kwame Nkrumah in Ghana, Jomo Kenyatta in Kenya, and Nelson Mandela in South Africa emerged during this period. These leaders galvanized their respective nations, mobilizing people to resist colonial oppression and fight for freedom. The independence movements were a significant catalyst for political consciousness and the assertion of African identity.

Pan-Africanism: The ideology of Pan-Africanism, which advocates for the unity and solidarity of African people, has played a pivotal role in shaping generations in Africa. Figures like Marcus Garvey, W.E.B. Du Bois, and Kwame Nkrumah popularized the concept, emphasizing the need for African nations to come together to address common challenges and promote socioeconomic development.

Apartheid in South Africa: The apartheid regime in South Africa, which enforced racial segregation and discrimination, sparked significant resistance and activism. The struggle against apartheid, led by figures like Nelson Mandela, Desmond Tutu, and Steve Biko, united generations in a common fight for equality and justice. The eventual dismantling of apartheid marked a triumph for human rights and a significant milestone in African history.

Post-Independence Challenges: After gaining independence, many African nations faced numerous challenges, including political instability, economic disparities, and conflicts. Generations like the Baby Boomers and Generation X navigated these difficulties, working towards stability, peace, and socioeconomic development. They confronted issues such as corruption, weak governance, and economic inequalities, striving to overcome these obstacles and create prosperous societies.

Globalization and Technological Advancements: The advent of globalization and rapid technological advancements in the late 20th century and beyond had a profound impact on African generations. The introduction of the internet, mobile phones, and social media platforms revolutionized communication, connectivity, and access to information. This transformation empowered younger generations, such as Millennials and Gen Z, who embraced digital platforms and utilized technology to drive social change, economic innovation, and entrepreneurship.

Resource Exploitation and Environmental Concerns: Africa's vast natural resources have been a double-edged sword. While they hold the potential for economic development, their exploitation has often been accompanied by environmental degradation, social tensions, and economic imbalances. Generations across Africa have grappled with the challenge of managing and benefiting from these resources sustainably, recognizing the need for responsible resource extraction and environmental conservation.

These historical facts, among many others, have shaped the experiences, aspirations, and actions of African generations. They have influenced the trajectory of nations, the struggle for independence, the pursuit of social justice, and the response to contemporary challenges.

By understanding and appreciating these historical contexts, we gain deeper insights into the motivations, values, and contributions of each generation in Africa.

.

GENERATIONS IN MIDDLE EAST

The book "Generations" has had a significant impact on understanding and analyzing generational dynamics in various regions, including the Middle East. While specific data on the influence of the book in the Middle East may not be readily available, its conceptual framework and insights into generational patterns can be applied to the region's context. Let's explore the impact of different generations and their contributions across the Middle East.

The Silent Generation (1928-1945) in the Middle East witnessed the end of colonial rule and the emergence of independent nations. Many of them actively participated in the struggles for independence, shaping the political landscape of their respective countries. Leaders like Gamal Abdel Nasser in Egypt, Habib Bourguiba in Tunisia, and Ayatollah Khomeini in Iran played crucial roles in shaping their nations' destinies.

The Baby Boomers (1946-1964) in the Middle East experienced significant socio-political changes. They

91

witnessed the aftermath of decolonization, the rise of nationalist movements, and the Arab-Israeli conflicts. This generation played an instrumental role in building post-independence institutions and infrastructure, contributing to nation-building efforts across the region. They also grappled with challenges such as political instability, economic disparities, and the impacts of the global energy market.

Generation X (1965-1980) in the Middle East navigated a complex period characterized by political and social upheaval. They experienced events such as the Iranian Revolution, the Iran-Iraq War, the Gulf War, and the Lebanese Civil War. This generation witnessed the rise of political Islam and the emergence of non-state actors in the region. They actively engaged in political movements, social activism, and cultural expressions that sought to address societal challenges.

The Millennial Generation (1981-1996) in the Middle East grew up in a globalized and interconnected world. They were exposed to rapid technological advancements, social media, and the internet. This generation played a significant role in the Arab Spring uprisings, using social media platforms to mobilize protests and demand political reforms. They have also been at the forefront of advocating for social justice, human rights, and gender equality in the region.

Generation Z (born after 1997) in the Middle East is a generation that has grown up in a digital age, highly connected and influenced by social media platforms. They have been vocal about various issues, including climate change, social justice, and political participation. This generation has shown a strong inclination toward entrepreneurship and innovation, leveraging technology to drive social and economic change in the region.

In terms of the Middle East's economic landscape, each generation has made its mark. The Silent Generation witnessed the establishment of industries and infrastructure in newly independent nations. Baby Boomers contributed to economic growth through their involvement in sectors such as oil, construction, and finance. Generation X witnessed economic liberalization policies, privatization, and increased foreign investment. Millennials and Gen Z have embraced digital entrepreneurship, startups, and innovation as they adapt to the changing global economic landscape.

However, it is crucial to note that the Middle East is a diverse region with variations in socio-economic development and political stability across different countries. Each nation has its unique historical, cultural, and geopolitical context, which shapes the experiences and contributions of its generations.

It is also important to acknowledge that the Middle East faces numerous challenges, including political conflicts, socio-economic disparities, youth unemployment, and gender inequality. Each generation has grappled with these issues in their own way, with varying degrees of success and impact.

In conclusion, the Middle East's generations have played crucial roles in shaping the region's history, politics, and socio-economic development. While the book "Generations" may not have specific data regarding the Middle East, its framework and insights provide valuable tools for understanding the dynamics of generational interactions and the impact of generational shifts in the Middle East. By examining historical events, social movements, and economic trends, we can gain a deeper understanding of how each generation has influenced the region.

The Silent Generation in the Middle East witnessed the transition from colonial rule to independence. In countries like Egypt, Tunisia, and Iran, leaders from this generation emerged as prominent figures in the struggle for self-determination. Gamal Abdel Nasser, for example, played a pivotal role in Egypt's quest for independence and later became a champion of Arab nationalism. The Silent Generation's contributions were vital in establishing the foundations of newly formed nations, shaping their political structures, and laying the groundwork for subsequent generations.

The Baby Boomers in the Middle East experienced a period marked by political turmoil, regional conflicts, and social changes. They were witnesses to the Arab-Israeli conflicts, the rise of pan-Arabism, and the aftermath of the Six-Day War. This generation played significant roles in politics, academia, and various industries. Leaders like King Hussein of Jordan and King Hassan II of Morocco, both Baby Boomers, navigated complex political landscapes and sought to maintain stability in their countries. Additionally, this generation contributed to economic growth, particularly through the development of the oil industry in the Gulf countries.

Generation X in the Middle East faced unique challenges as they came of age during a time of regional conflicts and geopolitical shifts. They witnessed the Iranian Revolution, the Iran-Iraq War, and the Lebanese Civil War, among other significant events. This generation, characterized by their resilience and adaptability, has played active roles in various fields. They have contributed to the arts, literature, journalism, and human rights activism. Notable figures like Orhan Pamuk, the Turkish novelist and Nobel laureate, and El Seed, the Tunisian street artist, exemplify the creative and impactful contributions of Generation X in the Middle East.

The Millennial Generation in the Middle East grew up in an era of globalization, digital connectivity, and social change. They were at the forefront of the Arab Spring, using social media platforms to mobilize protests and demand political reforms. This generation embraced entrepreneurship, technological advancements, and activism to bring about social justice and societal change. Young leaders like Malala Yousafzai from Pakistan and Mohammed bin Salman from Saudi Arabia represent the diverse pursuits and aspirations of this generation.

Generation Z in the Middle East is still coming of age, but they are already making their presence felt. This digitally native generation is characterized by their activism, environmental consciousness, and emphasis on social justice. They are harnessing technology to advocate for causes such as climate change, gender equality, and human rights. Notable young activists like Greta Thunberg and Malala Yousafzai serve as inspirations for this generation as they strive to shape a better future.

In terms of the Middle East's economic landscape, each generation has played a role in its development.

The Silent Generation participated in nation-building and the establishment of key industries. The Baby Boomers contributed to economic growth, particularly through the exploitation of oil resources. Generation X witnessed economic reforms, privatization, and foreign investment. Millennials and Generation Z are embracing digital entrepreneurship, innovation, and the gig economy as they navigate a rapidly changing global economic landscape.

However, it is important to note that the Middle East is a diverse region with varying levels of socio-economic development and political stability. Each country faces unique challenges and opportunities, and the impact of generations differs across the region.

In summary, the generations in the Middle East have left indelible marks on the region's history, politics, and socio-economic development. Through their contributions in leadership, activism, entrepreneurship, and innovation, they have shaped the trajectory of their respective countries and influenced societal change. Understanding the dynamics of generational shifts provides us with valuable insights into the Middle East's past, present, and future.

The impact of these generations extends beyond politics and economics. They have also shaped the social and cultural fabric of the region. Each generation has its own set of values, beliefs, and aspirations, which have influenced societal norms and behaviors.

For example, the Silent Generation, with its experiences of colonialism and struggle for independence, instilled a sense of nationalism and patriotism among the subsequent generations. They laid the groundwork for a strong sense of national identity and unity, which still resonates today.

The Baby Boomers, having witnessed the Arab-Israeli conflicts and regional instabilities, developed a strong focus on stability and security. They prioritized education and career advancement as means of building a prosperous future for their families. This emphasis on education led to significant advancements in the Middle East's educational systems, producing a highly educated workforce.

Generation X, marked by its exposure to political upheavals and social changes, developed a more questioning and critical mindset. They challenged traditional norms and institutions, pushing for greater freedoms, social justice, and gender equality. This generation saw a rise in activism, particularly among women's rights advocates, human rights defenders, and cultural innovators.

The Millennial Generation, growing up in an era of globalization and technological advancements, embraced the opportunities and challenges of an interconnected world. They are known for their adaptability, entrepreneurial spirit, and embrace of digital technologies. Millennials in the Middle East played a significant role in the Arab Spring uprisings, using social media platforms to mobilize protests and demand political change.

Generation Z, the youngest generation, is still in the process of defining its identity and impact.

However, they are already demonstrating a strong commitment to social and environmental issues. This generation is characterized by their digital nativism, environmental awareness, and focus on social justice. They are using their voices and platforms to advocate for a more sustainable and inclusive future.

Economically, the impact of these generations is evident in the region's development and growth. The Middle East has experienced rapid urbanization, infrastructural advancements, and diversification of economies. Each generation has contributed to these changes in different ways, whether through entrepreneurship, technological innovations, or investments in sectors such as renewable energy and tourism.

However, it is important to acknowledge that the Middle East faces challenges in terms of socio-economic disparities, unemployment, and political stability. While certain segments of society have enjoyed economic prosperity, others continue to struggle with poverty and lack of opportunities. Addressing these issues requires a comprehensive approach that considers the needs and aspirations of all generations.

I can conclude that, the impact of generations in the Middle East cannot be understated. Each generation has played a unique role in shaping the region's history, politics, economy, and culture.

From the struggles for independence to the embrace of digital technologies, they have left a lasting imprint on the Middle East's trajectory.

Understanding the experiences and contributions of these generations provides valuable insights into the region's past, present, and future, and allows for a more nuanced understanding of the challenges and opportunities that lie ahead.

GENERATIONAL STORYTELLING: BRIDGING THE GAP ACROSS AGES

In a world where time weaves together the tapestry of human existence, generations stand as chapters in the ever-evolving narrative of our collective history. Each generation brings forth a unique set of values, experiences, and perspectives that shape the way we navigate the world. And within this tapestry, lies the power of generational storytelling—a means to bridge the gap across ages, fostering understanding, empathy, and connection.

From the bustling coffee shops to the vibrant family gatherings, the stories of intergenerational encounters unfold. Let us embark on a journey through ten captivating glimpses into the lives of fictional characters, each representing a distinct generation. These stories paint a vivid picture of how different generations coexist, learn from one another, and contribute to the rich tapestry of human experiences.

In the bustling coffee shop, Sarah, the tech-savvy Gen Z student, sits next to Harold, the wise Silent Generation gentleman. While Sarah is immersed in the world of smartphones and social media, Harold finds solace in the traditional pleasures of flipping through a newspaper. Their presence beside one another speaks volumes—two different worlds intersecting in perfect harmony, a testament to the beauty of coexistence and mutual respect.

The family gathering is a hub of lively conversations and diverse perspectives. Emma, the free-spirited Millennial, ignites a spirited debate on climate change with her Baby Boomer parents. Amidst differing viewpoints, the love and shared passion for a better world become the common ground where understanding and unity thrive. It is within these family connections that generational wisdom is passed down and a collective desire for progress takes root.

Within the confines of a bustling office, Lisa, the detail-oriented Gen X professional, collaborates seamlessly with James, the ambitious Gen Y entrepreneur. Their unique work styles, rooted in the values of their respective generations, blend harmoniously, fostering innovation and success. It is through this collaboration that generational diversity becomes a catalyst for growth, a testament to the power of embracing different strengths.

The art exhibition showcases the creative expression of Mia, the imaginative Gen Alpha artist, and catches the eye of Michael, the Gen X art connoisseur. Mia's vibrant digital artwork merges traditional techniques with digital prowess, capturing the essence of a generation born into a world defined by technology. Michael, with his appreciation for the fusion of art forms, recognizes the evolution of artistic expression across generations, bridging the gap between analog and digital realms.

Communities thrive when individuals from different generations come together to make a difference. The neighborhood cleanup event unites Tom, the civic-minded Baby Boomer, and Lily, the eco-conscious Gen Z volunteer. Through shared stories and strategies, they work side by side, instilling a sense of responsibility towards the environment and inspiring future generations to preserve the planet.

Technology becomes a conduit for connection as Ethan, the patient Gen Y teacher, offers a smartphone tutorial to George, the curious Silent Generation gentleman. Through their interaction, a world once foreign and intimidating to George becomes accessible, creating new avenues for communication and connection across generations.

Entrepreneurship flourishes as Sarah, the driven Millennial entrepreneur, seeks guidance from Olivia, the seasoned Gen X business owner. Olivia imparts invaluable insights and mentors Sarah, sparking her entrepreneurial spirit and setting her on a path to success. It is within these mentoring relationships that generations intertwine, passing on knowledge and fostering the growth of future leaders.

Social activism rallies bring together the impassioned voices of Maya, the Gen Z activist, and Rebecca, the fervent Baby Boomer advocate. Their shared commitment to social justice transcends generational boundaries, uniting different perspectives in a powerful movement for change. It is through these collective efforts that generations stand together, amplifying their impact and creating lasting societal transformations.

EPILOGUE:
A TAPESTRY OF GENERATIONS

As we come to the end of our journey through the generations, we are left with a tapestry woven together by the experiences, aspirations, and impact of each cohort. From the Silent Generation to Generation Alpha, we have witnessed the remarkable evolution of societies, nations, and the world at large. We have explored how each generation has shaped history, leaving an indelible mark on the socio-political, economic, and cultural landscape of their respective regions.

Across continents, generations have faced diverse challenges and seized opportunities that have defined their era. The Silent Generation, marked by the aftermath of World War II, rebuilt shattered societies and laid the foundation for the prosperity that followed. The Baby Boomers, with their idealism and desire for change, challenged societal norms and transformed the world through their activism and cultural revolution. Generation X navigated the complexities of globalization and set the stage for the digital age. The Millennials harnessed the power of technology to connect and mobilize, reshaping political landscapes and driving social change. And Generation Z, with their digital nativism and unwavering commitment to social justice, have already begun to leave their imprint on a world desperately in need of their vision.

But what lies ahead for the coming generations? What challenges and opportunities will they face as they step onto the world stage? As we look to the future, it is clear that these generations will be tasked with addressing complex global issues that transcend borders and ideologies. Climate change, technological advancements, income inequality, and political instability are just a few of the pressing concerns that demand their attention.

However, amidst these challenges, there is reason for hope. The resilience, creativity, and determination displayed by previous generations serve as beacons of inspiration. Each generation has built upon the successes and failures of their predecessors, pushing boundaries and defying expectations. They have shown us that change is possible, that progress can be achieved, and that a brighter future is within our grasp.

The future will require collaboration and understanding between generations, as they navigate the complexities of an interconnected world. The wisdom of the Silent Generation, the drive of the

Baby Boomers, the pragmatism of Generation X, the idealism of the Millennials, and the passion of Generation Z will all play a vital role in shaping the world to come. By harnessing their collective strengths, they can forge a path forward that is sustainable, inclusive, and equitable.

The challenges they face will require innovative solutions, bold leadership, and a deep sense of empathy. It is imperative that they harness the power of technology and embrace its potential for positive change. They must confront the urgent need for environmental sustainability, working towards a greener and more sustainable future. They must champion social justice, equality, and diversity, ensuring that no one is left behind in the pursuit of progress.

As we close this book, we leave behind a legacy of generations who have shaped the world in remarkable ways. Their contributions, whether through political movements, scientific breakthroughs, artistic expressions, or acts of compassion, have left an indelible mark on the human story. We pass the baton to the coming generations, with the hope that they will carry the torch of progress, ignite new ideas, and create a world that is better, brighter, and more harmonious.

It is a future that holds immense potential, where the voices of the young and old converge to build bridges and foster understanding. It is a future where generations collaborate, learn from one another, and embrace the power of diversity. It is a future where the collective wisdom and shared experiences of the past serve as guiding lights, illuminating the path ahead.

And so, as we embark on this journey towards the future, let us remember the lessons learned from the generations that came before us. Let us honor their legacy by working together, transcending generational divides, and embracing the power of unity. Let us recognize that the challenges we face are not insurmountable but rather opportunities for growth and transformation.

In this tapestry of generations, we find hope, resilience, and the capacity for change. We see the potential to address the pressing issues of our time and create a world that is more just, inclusive, and sustainable. The task ahead may be daunting, but with the collective strength of generations, we can rise to the occasion.

As we look to Africa, the Middle East, and Russia, we see unique stories of struggle and triumph, of progress and setbacks. We witness the transformative power of generations in shaping the destiny of these regions. From the fight against colonialism and apartheid to the quest for independence and self-determination, the generations of Africa have paved the way for a brighter future.

In the Middle East, generations have experienced the complexities of geopolitics, the quest for peace, and the struggle for human rights. From the Arab Spring to ongoing conflicts, these generations have sought to forge a path towards stability, justice, and prosperity.

In Russia, generations have witnessed the fall of empires, the rise of communism, and the transition towards democracy. They have navigated economic challenges, political transformations, and the pursuit of social progress. Each generation has left an indelible mark on the nation's history and shaped its trajectory.

Economically, these regions have faced unique challenges and opportunities. From the rich natural resources of Africa to the oil-rich economies of the Middle East and the industrial might of Russia, generations have grappled with the complexities of development, inequality, and the distribution of wealth. The struggle for economic prosperity, coupled with the pursuit of social justice, has shaped the aspirations and actions of generations.

In the midst of these challenges, the impact on the lives of individuals, both rich and poor, cannot be overlooked. The generations have witnessed the rise of a middle class, the fight against poverty, and the pursuit of equality. They have experienced the disparities in access to education, healthcare, and opportunities. Generations have played pivotal roles in advocating for change, demanding social reforms, and working towards a more inclusive society.

The future for these regions lies in the hands of the coming generations. It is a future that requires visionary leadership, innovative solutions, and a deep commitment to human rights and sustainable development. It is a future where the voices of youth are amplified, where women are empowered, and where the marginalized are uplifted.

The challenges ahead may seem daunting, but history has shown that generations have the power to shape the course of nations. Through their collective actions, they can build bridges of understanding, foster peace and stability, and create environments where prosperity is shared by all.

As we close this book, let us reflect on the power of generations and their profound impact on the world. Let us acknowledge the interplay between historical events, societal changes, and the aspirations of individuals within the larger context of generations. May we be inspired by the stories of resilience, courage, and determination that have emerged from Africa, the Middle East, and Russia.

In the tapestry of generations, we find a shared humanity, interconnected by our hopes and dreams for a better world. Let us embrace the lessons of the past, honor the present, and look towards the future with optimism, knowing that the actions we take today will shape the world for generations to come.

Together, let us continue to weave the story of generations, leaving behind a legacy of progress, compassion, and unity.
The journey continues, and the future awaits us all.

ACKNOWLEDGMENTS

I wish I could simply say that I owe my gratitude only to myself and my unwavering belief in the beauty of others, in the stories I love to tell and narrate.

But that wouldn't be true: there have always been and will always be those who have helped me, and I genuinely feel grateful to each and every one of them in a single embrace... across generations.

It is only by combining our skills that we can continue to pass down stories and convey how we have lived and how we are living to future generations.

REVIEW, PLEASE

If you have made it this far, if you haven't given up, if this book has clarified for you what we have been, what we are, and what we could become...
Please leave a review and talk about it with your friends, family.
Spread the word, please.

Grazie, Amanda

Made in the USA
Las Vegas, NV
18 June 2023